My House

My House

Written by Patricia Jensen
Illustrated by Wayne Becker

My First
READER

children's press®

A Division of Scholastic Inc.

New York Toronto London Auckland Sydney
Mexico City New Delhi Hong Kong
Danbury, Connecticut

Library of Congress Cataloging-in-Publication Data

Jensen, Patricia.
  My house / written by Patricia Jensen ; illustrated by Wayne Becker.–
1st American.
        p. cm. – (My first reader)
Summary: Parts of houses old and new are mixed up and repainted red and
blue.
  ISBN 0-516-22934-6 (lib. bdg.)   0-516-24636-4 (pbk.)
  [1. Dwellings–Fiction. 2. Stories in rhyme.] I. Becker, Wayne, ill.
II. Title. III. Series.
  PZ8.3.J424My 2003
  [E]–dc21
                                    2003003639

CHILDREN'S PRESS and associated logos are trademarks and or registered trademarks of Scholastic Library Publishin
SCHOLASTIC and associated logos are trademarks and or registered trademarks of Scholastic Inc.

1 2 3 4 5 6 7 8 9 10 R 12 11 10 09 08 07 06 05 04 03

Note to Parents and Teachers

Once a reader can recognize and identify the 16 words
used to tell this story, he or she will be able to read successfully
the entire book. These 16 words are repeated throughout the story,
so that young readers will be able to easily recognize
the words and understand their meaning.

The 16 words used in this book are:

and	make
blue	my
doors	new
floors	old
has	paint
house	red
instead	the
is	your

My house is red.

Your house is blue.

My house is old.

Your house is new.

My old red house

has new blue doors.

Your new blue house

has old red floors.

Paint the old house.

Paint the new doors.

Paint the new house.

Paint the old floors.

Make your house old.

Make my house new.

Make your house red.

Make my house blue.

The new blue house

is old and red.

The old red house

is blue instead!

ABOUT THE AUTHOR

Patricia Jensen lives in New Jersey, has five children, three dogs, and is a stay-at-home mom.

ABOUT THE ILLUSTRATOR

Wayne Becker was born in Chicago, Illinois. After earning degrees at Northwestern University and the University of Michigan, he studied art at the School of Visual Arts in New York. Becker has been illustrating books and working in animation for more than thirty years. He lives in rural upstate New York with his wife, who was his high school sweetheart, and his dog.